THE DISSOLVE

A Simple Method
for Dissolving
What Holds You Back

Laurie McGinley

The Dissolve © Copyright 2026 Laurie McGinley

For more information, visit https://lauriemcginley.com/

ISBN: 979-8-9927329-2-4 (paperback)
ISBN: 979-8-9927329-3-1(ebook)

Edited by Rachel Warmath
Cover design and typesetting by Paperwing Studio
Cover background image: Unsplash

Dedication

This book is for you. You who works so hard, who cares so much, who tracks all the details, who is thoughtful before you act, who acts before you think, who picks up the things no one else wants to carry, who ensures integrity even when no one else is watching.

You are not all the same, nor are you motivated by the same things. What you have in common is that you are highly ambitious, wicked smart, and will not quit.

Contents

The Power Promise

Every person I have ever coached has had
a moment, whether quiet or catastrophic,
when something inside them whispered,
"I can't keep living like this."

That thought crossing your mind
does not mean you are weak. It means
you are waking up to the truth.

This book is here to show you that stuckness is
not a flaw in your character. It is a pattern that
formed long before you knew how to question it.

A pattern you learned. A pattern you
practiced. And a pattern you can dissolve.

The promise of this book is simple and profound. You will learn how to stop fighting yourself and live in a more authentic way.

Our goal here is not to force anything, and you don't even need to focus on building better routines or new coping skills. This is not a book about fixing your life.

You're simply going to work on building a relationship with yourself that doesn't contain so much pressure, so you can be present with yourself and see the possibilities that are all around you.

This is a book about reclaiming the power you always had and learning how to move with it instead of against it.

If you are tired of white knuckling your potential, if you are exhausted by your own brilliance, if you feel the cost of always managing yourself instead of expressing yourself, then welcome.

You belong here. This is where we begin.

Introduction

Why You Feel Stuck (and Why It Is Not Your Fault)

"Everything is scary when you have no visibility," Jon Stewart once told Stephen Colbert. He was talking about sea creatures. But he might as well have been talking about the human nervous system.

When you cannot see potential attacks, everything feels threatening.

That is the secret no one tells you about burnout,
overwhelm, procrastination, perfectionism,
and overachievement. They are not personality
traits. They are survival strategies.

They are invisible barriers that once
protected you and now limit you.

You learned to perform. You learned to push. You
learned to disappear. You learned to over-function.

You learned to outrun your own brilliance.

Not because you were broken. Because these
strategies worked... until they did not.

The people who come to me for coaching
are not weak. They are founders, visionaries,
executives, parents, geniuses, and investors.
They are powerful people who have learned to
weaponize their own drive against themselves.

They do not burn out because they lack ability.
They burn out because their old strategies
cannot carry the weight of their next becoming.

Here is the most important truth you need
to know before we go any further:

You are not stuck because you are failing.
You are stuck because you are evolving.

Your old identity cannot take you
where you want to go.

Your invisible barriers know that, and they
are sounding every alarm they have.

This book will teach you a new
way to move, like this:

Name It.

Reveal the invisible barrier running the show.

Soften It.

Shift from threat to presence.

Sashay Through It.

Rehearse the version of you that can move freely.

As you read this book, you will be invited to try this new method of moving, and you will likely begin to feel the difference right away.

This isn't an abstract idea, but rather something you'll feel in your muscles, your breath, your posture, your choices, your conversations, your relationships, and your leadership.

The Dissolve™ is something you live, not something you memorize.

So, take a breath. Set down the pressure to get this right. You do not need to perform your way through this book. You only need to be present.

Because once you can see the invisible, nothing about your life stays the same.

Let's begin.

Chapter 1

The Anatomy of Being Stuck

You are not broken.

You are trapped behind invisible barriers.

You used to be able to do what you are trying to do now. You used to have more energy, more motivation, and more concentration. And yet here you are, aware that something feels heavier than it should, but unable to locate the source.

What if you're not broken at all? What if you're simply navigating unseen limits?

Every high performer carries them. Invisible barriers. Internal patterns that once protected you but now restrict you. They shape how you think, how you act, and how you feel. They hum beneath your decisions. They frame what you attempt and what you avoid. And because they operate beneath awareness, they blend in with the rest of who you are.

You often mislabel them as:

- Stress
- Burnout
- Anxiety
- Procrastination
- Overwhelm

But the reality of what's happening is more subtle.

Invisible barriers are protection systems your nervous system adopted long ago. Some act like governors, restricting your speed so you never outrun what once felt safe. Others act like inner judges or drivers or guardians. Their roles differ, but their impact does not. Every invisible barrier limits your access to the truest version of yourself.

They keep you safe. They also keep you small. And if you are a high achiever, once you understand the mechanics of these barriers, you can dissolve them. You can take the governor off your system. You can reclaim the power that has always been yours.

The fact that you are reading this book tells me you are already ready for that shift.

My Early Invisible Barriers

My own invisible barriers showed up long before I ever understood what they were.

I was thirteen, flying through the air at a middle school track meet. High jump had always felt like controlled falling—the sprint toward the bar, the plant, the arc over it, the inevitable crash into the mat on the other side.

That day, something wasn't quite right.

The moment when the sprint turns into a jump and one foot takes all the pressure didn't feel the same. It hurt. But not enough to stop, I told myself. Not enough to matter. It wasn't like I couldn't still jump.

So I kept jumping. I still ran at practice and I kept training through the rest of the season.

It wasn't until a year later, when I finally saw a doctor, that I learned I'd been competing on a broken foot the entire time. The X-ray showed the fracture clearly—an injury that should have sidelined me immediately.

"How did you not know?" the doctor asked.

I didn't have an answer then. But I do now.

Pain wasn't information to me. It was background noise. Something to override, ignore, push through. I had already learned, somewhere deep in my wiring, that slowing down was more dangerous than breaking myself.

That if I stopped, I would disappear.

Years later, in my undergraduate architecture studio, I met another repetition of that same pattern.

We were tasked with building a massive topographic model of Minneapolis, the kind of project that required slicing hundreds of

cardboard contours by hand, layering them
to create the rise and fall of the city's terrain.
It was tedious, meticulous work. The kind
that demanded precision and patience.

I had neither.

What I had was an X-Acto knife, a cutting mat,
and a burning need to prove I belonged there.

So I worked. Hour after hour, day after day.
My right index finger gripped that knife so
tightly that by the end of the first week, the
tendon began to throb. By the second week,
I couldn't fully straighten it. By the third,
every cut sent a sharp ache up my forearm.

I didn't stop.

I told myself it was dedication.
Discipline. The price of excellence.

But really, it was fear disguised as work ethic.

The model was beautiful. It had clean
lines and perfect contours. The kind of
work that earned quiet nods of approval
from professors who rarely gave them.

But inside, I had pulverized myself for worthiness.

I had taken my terror of not being enough
and compressed it into my finger until
something inside me broke—again.

That was the moment I began to see the pattern.

It's not that I was a failure, or that I was weak, but
I had been carrying an invisible barrier for years.

I would later name her **The Overcrusher**. She
was the part of me that believed the harder I
worked, the more I could prove myself and earn
my place. She thought anything less than total
self-sacrifice was laziness in disguise. And when I
really thought about it, she had been with me long
before the architecture studio or the broken foot.

This is what most high achievers do.

We call it discipline, or drive, or commitment.

But beneath the surface, it is fear
disguised as excellence.

A Lot of Brilliant People Have the Same Pattern

When I began guiding executives, politicians,
founders, investors, leaders, and innovators,
I saw the same pattern again and again.

Brilliant people, trapped behind invisible barriers.

People capable of moving entire industries,
but unable to move themselves. These were
people who could solve any external problem
but could not escape their internal ones.

What stops high achievers is rarely a lack of skill
or intelligence. It is mismanaged motivation.
It is devotion hardened into fear. It is a
survival strategy turning into a limitation.

Invisible barriers are not weaknesses.
They are old solutions still running long
after their usefulness has expired.

Meet Sarah, a Perfectionist

For Sarah, her invisible barrier showed up
as perfectionism with a moral shine to it.

Her spreadsheets were immaculate, and her home was perfectly organized and curated so that the moment you walked in the door, you felt a sense of how successful and capable she was seeing the way her pillows lined up on the couch, and how all of the color schemes in each room were coordinated.

People loved working with her. She had a reputation for being dependable and thorough, and she held tightly to keeping up that reputation. She was the person who never dropped a ball, never missed a deadline, never let anything slip through the cracks.

But she was exhausted.

"I feel like I'm trying to protect what matters to me, but it's shredding me in the process," she said. "Like being excellent while crawling through barbed wire." Her eyes were glassy, but her posture was still composed, like always.

Her problem was not how much she did. It was that her idea of enough had no edges. Her invisible barrier was an internal judge named Haras—her name spelled backwards, because that's what this voice felt like, the inverse of the encouraging voice inside her.

Haras told her:

- If you slow down, someone will be harmed.
- If you rest, you are letting standards slip.
- Even when you succeed, you should have done better.

Sarah's integrity had turned into control.
And control had turned into suffering.

Jonah's Magnetism

Jonah looked completely different.

He was magnetic. Fast thinking. Fast moving.
An award-winning creative director who
lived at a pace that left people breathless.
His situation did not look like stuckness.
Surprisingly, it looked like success.

But inside, he was drowning.

"If I stop, it all falls apart," he told me. "If I stop moving, I might not be relevant anymore."

His invisible barrier was the Clock Demon. Not a governor that slowed him down, but a driver that had him making mistakes and missing

opportunities. A force that kept him moving so
quickly he couldn't even feel his emotions.

The Clock Demon told Jonah:
- Your worth is based on how productive you are.
- You are already behind.
- You are working on the wrong thing. Move
  faster.

Sarah controlled everything around her because
she believed that's what kept her safe. Jonah
kept moving at breakneck speed because he
believed that's what made him matter.

Different barriers. Same anatomy.
Both of them had turned their fear into
something that looked like a strength.

A Small, Survivable Life

Burnout is not depletion. Burnout is containment.
It is brilliance compressed into a life that is
too small for you. It is ambition forced into
predictability. It is potential throttled by patterns
that once protected you but now restrict you.

The Enneagram, a system that identifies
nine distinct ways people are wired to see
and move through the world, helped me see
these patterns earlier and more clearly: Ones
like Sarah use their sense of right/wrong to
build a prison for themselves. Threes like
Jonah can't stop moving or achieving because
they think become irrelevant if they do.

Later on in the book, you'll meet two other
characters, too. Like Maya, who is a Five. Fives
gather so much knowledge and information
before acting that they often fail to show
up. They get stuck in analysis paralysis.

You'll also meet Kai, who is an Eight. They use
power to avoid being hurt. Kai believed being
strong meant staying in control, so his power
became a wall between him and everyone else.

These are different stories with different
Enneagram types but they all show how
motivation can be turned into a trap.
You do not need to know anything about
the Enneagram to see yourself in these
characters and their experiences.

Enneagram Types You'll See in This Book

The Enneagram is a map of nine distinct motivational patterns. It gives us nine ways of seeing the world, making meaning, and moving through challenges. Unlike personality traits or behavioral profiles, the Enneagram illuminates the deeper motivation beneath your actions. It reveals the internal driver that shapes your attention, your habits, and your stress responses.

One (Sarah): The Perfectionist

Driven by a need to be good, responsible, and upright. Ones strive for integrity but often confuse relentless effort with moral virtue. Under stress, they tighten, overcorrect, and carry more than is theirs. Their growth path is softening into gentleness, presence, and shared responsibility.

Three (Jonah): The Hero

Motivated by excellence, recognition, and doing what works. Threes move fast, produce constantly, and shape shift to meet expectations. Their invisible barrier is overidentifying with performance and losing access to rest and authenticity. Their growth path is slowing down enough to feel themselves again.

Five (Maya): The Researcher

Fueled by curiosity, depth, and inner mastery. Fives tend to withdraw into their mind, conserving energy and avoiding overwhelm. Their barrier is disappearing or disengaging when others cannot track their thinking. Their growth path is staying present in connection while still honoring their clarity.

Eight (Kai): The Motivator

Motivated by autonomy, strength, and forward motion. Eights lead with intensity, vision, and instinct, often carrying the whole future on their shoulders. Their barrier is pushing harder when they feel vulnerable. Their growth path is learning that openness is not weakness. It is the source of their true power.

These summaries are not meant to teach the Enneagram in full. They are meant to orient you inside the stories you have just read. If you recognize yourself in one of these patterns, trust the resonance. If you do not, trust that

you will still find yourself in the universal
arc of dissolving what holds us back.

You Cannot Dissolve What You Cannot See

You cannot outwork an invisible barrier. You
cannot out-strategize it. You cannot outperform
the part of you that believes slowing down is
dangerous. You cannot smash through it.

But you can *name it*.

And once you name it, everything begins to move.

In the next chapter, you will watch Jonah call his
invisible barrier by name and see what happens
when his awareness breaks the spell. But before
we get there, I want to offer you an exercise to
try. You'll see these "Mini Dissolve" prompts
throughout the book. They're designed to give
you something actionable now to help you shift
the invisible barriers that are holding you back.

Mini Dissolve

Does one of these questions land close to home for you? Pick that one and consider the answer.

- Where are you mistaking effort for integrity?
- Where are you chasing progress to prove your worth?
- Where are you mistaking control for safety, and what would happen if you loosened your grip?
- Where are you hiding behind understanding because it feels safer than acting?
- Where are you mistaking freedom for escape?
- Where are you mistaking peace for silence instead of presence?

These questions are doorways that can lead you somewhere new.

How Do We Get Un-Stuck?

Stuckness always begins with good intentions. Every client I have worked with began with a desire to lead, to build something that mattered, and to take as big a bite out of life as they could handle. They did not fall into burnout because they were lazy or unmotivated. They fell because they cared so deeply that they leaned too far into the very strengths that once lifted them up.

Invisible barriers rarely appear in your weakness. They hide instead in a very sneaky place: your strengths.

Sarah's devotion to integrity made her unstoppable, yet it also made her unable to stop. Jonah's hunger for excellence made him magnetic, yet it also made him struggle with feeling like he could slow down and rest. Their brilliance came with blind spots that narrowed their lives.

It is not just Sarah and Jonah. All of us construct invisible barriers shaped by our wiring, fears, and experiences. For some, it is morality. For others, image or control or knowledge or peace. The form shifts, but the logic remains the same. If I stay on top of everything, I will be safe.

Except fear and being free do not coexist.

Early in my coaching work I used the term
the governor effect to describe one category
of invisible barrier. A governor limits output
by capping performance for the sake of safety.
Cars have them. Engines have them. Some high
achievers have them too. When I explained
this to Sarah the first time, she froze.

"You mean the part that is supposed to keep me
from crashing is the reason I cannot go anywhere?"

"Exactly," I told her.

Her system was organized around control. To
feel in control, she needed every detail, plan, and
standard to be set to a high bar of excellence.
She confused control with safety and could
not feel the difference. Control is loud and
tight. Safety is quiet and expansive. You cannot
hear safety when control is shouting over it.

Sarah's burnout did not come from working
too much. It came from resisting too much.
Every time life asked her to trust, she answered
with structure. Every time her body asked
for softness, she answered with strategy.

Then, The Dissolve began.

We slowed down and traced her pattern. Where did Haras appear? What triggered her? What did she fear? What did she protect Sarah from? Where did Sarah feel her presence in her body?

Sarah tried first to solve Haras logically. She created charts to track her emotional patterns. She asked for more practices, more routines, more ways to perform her way through the pain. But invisible barriers cannot be dissolved intellectually. They dissolve through relationship.

That is what naming does. It turns the barrier into something you can relate to rather than something that operates as if it is you.

When you cannot see your invisible barriers, they act like emotional bumpers. You wander too close to the edge of something unfamiliar, and they silently guide you back to what you already know. Picture an invisible shepherd herding your brilliant thoughts, actions, and desires into a narrow, predictable, and survivable path.

Invisible barriers do not only hold you back. They also shrink the world you inhabit.

When Sarah began seeing Haras as just a voice
and not something ruling her entire being,
something softened. She started noticing when
she had the thought, *you should be better*,
and would answer, *I am already enough*.

At first, it felt false. Then it felt
possible. Eventually, it felt true.

She entered a relationship with Haras
instead of living under her command. And
once she did, she could see how Haras had
been herding her brilliance into a life far
smaller than she was meant to live.

Success and Suffering

There is an irony at the heart of high-
achiever burnout. The same skills that create
success often create suffering. Discipline,
focus, and self-responsibility are powerful
tools until they harden into identity.

I remember when one of my own invisible barriers
revealed itself. During my graduate architecture
program, I worked on a project I loved. I gathered
drawings, information, images, and stories until

I was exhausted. When it came time to present, I spoke for more than thirty-five minutes without realizing it and completely lost the audience. I had armored myself with knowledge to protect against not being enough. My professor, Ozayr, gently suggested brevity the next time.

That was the moment I recognized my old barrier. I heard that voice that was so active in my mind, the one saying: *You have to prove your worthiness. Show them you have done more than enough.* The Overcrusher had returned in a new form.

My invisible barrier wasn't perfectionism. It was the constant need to prove my worth.

If I did not struggle, sacrifice, or push myself to the edge, I believed my work had no value. I believed I had no value. That motivation is what caused me to fall flat in delivering a project I adored.

This is the concealed truth of burnout culture. We are not addicted to achievement. We are addicted to suffering as evidence that we have earned our place.

Jonah drove himself into the ground through speed, meaning constant motion was the way he proved his worth. Sarah drove herself into the ground through perfectionism. It was like she needed to be relentless in how responsible she was all the time. And I drove myself into the ground through over-preparation. If I could just provide enough exhaustive effort, if I could do a little more, prove a little more... then I might be worthy.

Each of us carried the same root belief. If it feels easy, I'm not working hard enough, and everything could fall apart.

It is the biggest lie brilliant people tell themselves.

Stuck Is Feedback

The first dissolve is often the hardest because it requires a shift before you fully understand why. Sarah wanted to analyze her stuckness. Jonah wanted to outrun his. I wanted to outperform mine. None of those strategies worked.

When you stop seeing "I'm stuck" as a failure and begin seeing it as feedback, everything changes. You no longer have to push through the barrier. You can walk toward it. You can sit with it. You can ask what it is trying to protect.

When Sarah realized her invisible barrier
was not punishing her but protecting her, she
cried. Not from sadness. From recognition.

"It was trying to keep me safe," she told me.

"Yes," I said.

This part of you learned long ago that slowing
down or losing control or not proving yourself
was dangerous. It learned that mistakes were
shameful. It learned that softness was not safe.

You cannot punish a protector into
submission. You have to bring it home.

The Cave You Fear to Enter

If something inside you hums with recognition
as you read this, know that you are not behind.
You are standing at the doorway of awareness.

And as Joseph Campbell said, "The treasure
you seek lies in the cave you fear to enter."

Stuckness means your system is shielding
something precious. The question is what.

That is where we go next. You
must learn to Name It.

Because nothing dissolves until it is seen.

Mini Dissolve

What is your invisible barrier, or where do you get
stuck when you reach for what you want?

What is that barrier trying to protect you from?

Seeing Stuckness as an Invitation

Here is what I tell every client at this point.
Stuckness is not permanent, and you do not have
to keep living like this. Stuckness is not the end
of your story. It is an invitation to a new one.

A governor will slow you down when the
part of you that built your success senses
danger in expanding. It is the voice that
says, "Do not outgrow what made you safe.
Remember how hard it was last time."

Sarah had a governor whispering, "Stay good,
stay responsible, stay righteous." Jonah's
barrier said, "Stay visible, stay productive,
stay winning." Mine used to repeat, "Stay
useful, stay in overdrive, stay ahead."

None of these voices were malicious. They believed
they were protecting us from chaos or rejection or
shame. But protection that never turns off does
not remain protection. It becomes an invisible
barrier that limits the life you are allowed to live.

Most of my clients are people who can work
through anything *except themselves*. They
build careers on solving problems and clearing

obstacles. They move mountains before breakfast.
But when the obstacle is their own drive,
their usual tools stop working. Grit becomes
gasoline. Effort becomes exhaustion. What once
propelled them forward now buries them.

When Sarah slowed down enough to feel what
lived beneath her perfection, she discovered
something unexpected: fear of loss. She had spent
decades being reliable and righteous and excellent.
Underneath that identity lived a quiet sadness.
She did not know who she was when she was not
performing as the good person everyone expected
her to be. Her perfection was her protection. It
shielded the tenderness she never learned to trust.

That is the hidden cost of burnout. You
do not only lose energy. You lose identity.
You forget that who you are is good.

And paradoxically, fear of loss is often
the first sign that life is coming back.
It means the system is thawing.

Flooring It in the Sand

Every dissolve begins with disorientation. The old logic stops working. The strategy that always saved you, whether control or perfection or momentum, suddenly collapses. You cannot force your way forward. You also cannot return to the old pattern. Most people panic at this point and double down, which is the psychic equivalent of getting your car stuck in sand and flooring it. All you do is spin deeper into the rut.

Sarah's first dissolve moment happened on an ordinary Tuesday. She had over-promised on a project, over-delivered, and still felt unsatisfied. She sat in her car after work, hands on the wheel, heart pounding. No one was demanding anything of her. She was the one cracking the whip.

For the first time, she truly felt it: *I cannot keep living like this.*

The collapse moments were no longer restful. The tidy moments were no longer productive. The anxious moments scattered her so completely she could barely function.

That was the beginning. Not of burnout.
Burnout had been unfolding for years. The
beginning was awareness. A simple, quiet
truth. She saw the pattern. She named
the pain. And things began to move.

When you are stuck deep in sand, you
eventually realize you cannot get out alone.
Sarah reached that point. She had dug herself
in so thoroughly that the only reasonable
move was to stop pushing and ask for help.

A Mirror of Kindness

If this chapter is a mirror, I want you to see your
reflection without judgment. Maybe your invisible
barrier looks like planning without end. Maybe
it shows up as relentless achievement or people-
pleasing or overthinking. Maybe you have worn
it for so long that it feels like your personality.

You do not have to rip it out. You
only have to recognize it.

That is the first mercy of The Dissolve.

It's simple awareness. It does not
have to be an attack on yourself.

Sarah did not need to eradicate Haras. She needed
to understand her. Jonah did not need to destroy
the Clock Demon. He needed to learn its language.
I did not need to demolish the Overcrusher. I
needed to name the urge to perform worthiness.

Invisible barriers lose their power the moment
they are named. And in the chapters ahead,
you will learn the rhythm of this process:

1. Name It. Bring the invisible into awareness.

2. Soften It. Shift from resistance to
   relationship.

3. Sashay Through It. Move with ease, without
   force, with comfort and safety.

These steps sound simple. They *are* simple.
They do not require years of therapy, a wellness
retreat, or a dramatic life pause. They require
honesty and attention. They require willingness
to let go of what no longer protects you.

Name it and you break autopilot.

Soften it and you return to curiosity.

Sashay through it and you begin to
move like someone who is free.

This is the anatomy of becoming unstuck.

Reconnection

Months after her breakthrough Sarah
said, "It feels like my body trusts me again.
Like I actually *trust myself* again."

That is what The Dissolve restores. Not
perfection. Not productivity. Trust.

By the end of one session, she did not
glow with enlightenment or float into
transcendence. She simply looked relieved.
Human again. As if a weight had slid off one
shoulder and she could breathe fully again.

That is what I want for you. Not a reinvention of
your entire life. Not a motivational overhaul. Just
the relief of finding yourself beneath the noise.

This is the work I do every day. We bring the barriers into view, soften their grip, and teach your system a new way to move.

If you see yourself in Sarah or Jonah, stay close as you read. And if you realize at some point that you do not want to walk this alone, that is exactly what I am here for.

Mini Dissolve

What part of you is tired of protecting an outdated version of safety?

Chapter 2

Name It

The first step of The Dissolve feels deceptively
simple and impossibly hard at the same time.

Name it.

You cannot work with what you are not
aware of, and you cannot stay aware
of what you refuse to name.

Most of us are fluent in describing our
symptoms. Stress. Exhaustion. Overwhelm.
We can list the behaviors, but we rarely
call the barrier itself by its real name.

When I ask clients what is stopping them from having what they want, they often say, "I do not know. I am just stuck."

That word, stuck, is what it feels like when we cannot see the part of us behind the curtain, quietly pulling the strings of our own limitations.

Naming is the moment the curtain moves.

And you'll feel a shift in your body, too. Your forehead might relax. Your chest might soften, instead of feeling tight like it has for months. You might feel like you can truly take a deep breath, instead of feeling on edge. These are all good signs that your nervous system feels safe.

The Power in Naming It

Jonah pulled back the curtain on why he was stuck the moment he named it.

Jonah looked successful on paper—awards, clients, followers, the works. But he woke up every morning already feeling behind. When we traced the pattern beneath his exhaustion,

we found the belief driving everything: that
he needed to hurry up and achieve more, or
else he might be worthless. The day he named
it The Clock Demon, there was a shift.

Naming did not fix it. But naming revealed it.

Reveal

Naming turns an invisible force into
something you can point to instead of
something you are trapped inside of.

Naming it is like hearing a noise in a dark
basement and turning the lights on instead of
sprinting up the stairs convinced you are being
chased. The moment the light flips on, you
see it was only a hockey stick falling over.

The fear was real. The *cause* was not.

When Jonah named the Clock Demon, he
was not exaggerating. He was describing the
emotional truth of his experience. This unseen
force had been driving his entire life with no
pause, no softness, no room to breathe.

But once it had a name, it became smaller.
A *part* of him instead of *all* of him.

You cannot work with what you cannot
define. Once named, it becomes something
you can hold in your hands instead of
the storm that keeps you out at sea.

Sarah's Internal Auditor

Sarah's naming moment came later, and hers
sounded softer but landed just as hard.

We were in the middle of a conversation when
she said, almost casually, "It is like I have an
internal auditor always marking my work."

I asked, "What is their name?"

She laughed, thinking I was joking. When
she realized I was not, she went silent. After
a long moment she whispered, "Haras."

The name was the reverse of her own. A mirror
version of herself. The part of her that critiqued,
corrected, and controlled without rest.

As soon as she said the name, she saw the
truth. Haras never took breaks. Haras always
outran her. Haras kept her performing like
a puppet while she tried to keep up.

Once she named her, the relationship
shifted. She stopped being maneuvered
by Haras and started relating to her.

That is what naming does. It reveals the dynamic
of the unseen pattern you've been operating under.

Awareness Without Attack

Naming is not about diagnosing your
trauma or creating a new identity.

Naming is catching the moment your invisible
barrier has its hands on your strings and
gently saying, I see what you are doing.

That simple move is the first
softening of the armor.

Different people name their barriers differently.
For Ones like Sarah, it often sounds like

a moral judge. For Threes like Jonah, a timekeeper or performance coach. For Fives like Maya, an inner librarian urging more research before speaking. For Eights like Kai, a General who fears losing command.

Each name is a compass. It points toward the invisible barrier, and it points toward your gift[1].

Because invisible barriers always sit between you and the treasure you seek.

What You Are Missing

Jonah's gift was focus. He could distill chaos into clarity within minutes. But the Clock Demon twisted that gift into a grind. He moved so fast he ran right past the treasure he was meant to gather.

Sarah's gift was integrity. She sensed how everything mattered. But Haras convinced her that goodness required suffering. She pushed so hard she could not see her own brilliance.

---

1 If you'd like ideas of other invisible barriers, look in the exercises in the back of the book.

Once she named it, she began to
separate her conscience from her
compulsion. She cut the strings.

That is the heart of this work. You cannot
dissolve what you still confuse with identity.

If the invisible barrier is still pulling your
strings, you will repeat the same patterns, no
matter how hard you try to outgrow them.

Name It

Try this now. Instead of analyzing, simply listen.

When you think about what keeps you
stuck, what image or phrase rises first.
Do not make it poetic. Do not make it
respectable. Invisible barriers never are.

Maybe it is The Gatekeeper or
The Editor or The Fixer.

Maybe it is The Shadow Boss
or The Puppet Master.

Maybe it is The Credential Chaser
or The Overthinker.

Whatever it is, write it down. Say it
out loud. Notice what happens in your
body when you speak its name.

That is the beginning of The Dissolve.

Mini Dissolve

What name does your stuckness answer to?

See the exercise at the back of the book called
"How to Dissolve in 90 Seconds" for more
inspiration.

A True Name

When people start this work, they often
want to skip naming and jump straight
to fixing. Clients will say something to me
along the lines of, "Let's get to the solution
part. I want to move on. What do I do?"

I get it. Naming feels strange to smart, high-
achieving adults who spend their lives operating
through logic, strategy, and performance.
But Naming It is an act of leadership.

When you name something, you stop being
ruled by it. You become the one who assigns
meaning. You reclaim your agency.

That is why I tell clients to choose a true name.
It can actually feel quite uncomfortable or even
slightly embarrassing, and that's how you'll
know you're on the right track. Choosing a name
that really captures what's been holding you
back—that immediately disarms this invisible
barrier and brings you closer to dissolving it.

Meet Maya

Maya's naming moment was quieter.

She was deliberate, thoughtful, always
analyzing all the details before she would
speak. When she described her stuckness,
she used words like "fog" and "distance."

"I can't seem to share what I know
until it's complete," she said. "And
then the moment is gone."

I asked her to picture the part of her that holds
everything back while conversations move
past her. "What does it look like?" I said.

She closed her eyes and said, "She is like a
museum curator. She is always polishing the
glass but never lets anyone touch what is
inside. She will not let most pieces into the
gallery because they are too precious."

And that is when she named her
invisible barrier The Curator.

The Curator was careful. She believed she was
protecting Maya's brilliance and ensuring that

others wouldn't misunderstand her. But in her caution, she kept Maya isolated and silent.

When Maya spoke the name out loud, she smiled for the first time in weeks. "The Curator is not mean," she said softly. "She is just scared."

Naming transformed Maya's Curator from a fierce gatekeeper into someone she could start to work *with*, not against.

Rules

Once an invisible barrier has a name, it starts to reveal its rules.

Sarah's Haras had three core rules:

1. Never let standards drop.
2. Never need help.
3. Never rest while others suffer.

Jonah's Clock Demon's rules were all about speed. He demanded that Jonah keep moving fast, so he could keep feeling safe. His rule said that *if you are not producing, then you are falling behind.*

Maya's Curator lived by a simpler code:

1. Only share when complete.
2. Only speak when certain.
3. Only connect when there is no risk.

When these rules stay hidden, they run your life. But once spoken, they lose their authority. Like catching an overzealous volunteer running the entire event by accident, you can step in, redirect, and choose something different.

That is why naming is potent. It is the first act of rebellion against the invisible laws that govern your stuckness.

Whose Rules

A few weeks after Jonah named the Clock Demon, we were reviewing his schedule and he said, "I cannot take that afternoon off."

I asked, "Who said that? You or the Clock Demon?"

He laughed, caught in the act. "The Demon, he said. He is relentless."

"Good awareness," I told him. "Now that you can hear the difference, you can choose who drives."

This is what naming creates. Awareness becomes agency. You are no longer the puppet. You are the one holding the strings.

The goal is not to silence the invisible barrier. The goal is to know its voice so clearly that you never mistake it for your own again.

Naming is Evolution

There is something sacred about naming. Naming marks the beginning of relationship. You name what you are ready to meet.

When you name your stuckness, you acknowledge that this part of you has existed for a reason. It has tried to protect you, guide you, and keep you safe. It simply does not understand that you have outgrown its methods.

Naming is how you thank it for its service and invite it to evolve.

Meeting

Before we move to the next step, take a moment. Close your eyes. Feel where the invisible barrier lives in your body.

Now say its name. Not with anger. With recognition. With compassion.

If it helps, imagine turning toward it and saying, *I see you. I know you have been working hard. But I am ready for something new.*

That is the first dissolve. Not a fight. A meeting.

Mini Dissolve

Say the name of your invisible barrier out loud. What changes in your body when you do?

Naming as a Practice

Naming an invisible barrier is not a one-time
revelation. It is a practice. Each time you catch
the voice, you call it what it is. Each time you
notice the familiar tightening in your chest
or jaw, you whisper its name. Naming is how
you move from unconsciously merging with
the barrier to consciously relating to it.

When Jonah began naming the Clock Demon
regularly, he noticed it in places he had never
thought to look. The way he checked his phone at
red lights. The urge to leave his chair in the middle
of meetings. The panic that rose when he did not
have an immediate project to chase. Each moment
became a quiet opportunity to say, There you are.

At first it felt strange, even performative.
But slowly, the dynamic shifted.

One day he said to me, "I think the Clock
Demon is relaxing. He still shows up, but
I do not run when he shouts anymore."

That is when you know naming has done its
work. Naming moves you from possession
to partnership. The invisible barrier does

not vanish. It simply stops gripping the
wheel with white-knuckled control.

Remember, invisible barriers are compasses
that distract you from the treasure you seek.
When you shift into relationship with them, you
become the student. You begin to understand
what has been blocking your success and why.

Imagine having a map to that treasure.
Naming is how the map begins to appear.

"Shoulds"

Sarah's relationship with Haras evolved
just as visibly. In the beginning, Haras
sounded rigid, fixed, like it was rattling off
commandments: "Be better. Be right. Be more."

But when she finally named the voice, she began
to hear the fear underneath the "shoulds."

She kept a sticky note on her desk that
read, "*Haras* speaks in shoulds."

Whenever she caught herself thinking, I *should*
send another email or I *should* stay later, she would

pause and breathe. Sometimes she whispered,
"Thank you, Haras. I can handle this now."

Naming gave her permission to
reclaim her own choices.

Talking Back

Maya discovered that the Curator had
a sense of humor. Once she recognized
the voice that told her to keep polishing
her ideas, she started talking back.

"The exhibit is closed," she would say
with a grin when she caught herself
editing an email for the twelfth time.

Her work did not get sloppier. It actually got
better. She felt more alive. She collaborated
more freely, without worrying so much what
other people would think. Her brilliance
became a conversation rather than a
perfectly curated museum display.

That is one of the gifts of naming. It introduces
play where there used to be pressure.

Into the Light

Across every client, the practice is the same.

First you Name it. Then you Notice it. And every
time it appears, you let it know you see it.

You don't have to punish that part of you
or repress it. We're not trying to do an
exorcism here. Just offer recognition.

The nervous system cannot transform under
attack, but it can transform under awareness.
Naming brings the invisible barrier into
the light where it can soften and shift.

Messy

The first dissolve often happens using language. You
may not feel different right away. In fact, you might
feel worse for a moment, like you opened a window
in a long-closed room and stirred up the dust.

That is normal. Awareness is messy.

The discomfort is a sign that you are waking
up from an old pattern. If it felt comfortable,

it would only be more of what you already
know. And as you know, the pasture is safe for
the sheep, but it also keeps them contained.

The more often you name it, the
faster you reclaim your power.

Jonah said it well. It is not about
censoring the Clock Demon into silence.
It is about shortening the amount of time
he runs on and pulls my strings.

Yes!

That is progress. That is the beginning of freedom.

Remember, the Clock Demon is a part of
Jonah, just like your governor is a part of you.
The more you ignore, suppress, or argue with
an invisible barrier, the louder it becomes.
These parts tighten when you attack them.
But they relax when they are acknowledged.

Greetings

If you have named your invisible barrier, write the
name somewhere you will see it. Not as a warning,

but as a reminder that you are the one steering now.

When the voice pipes up again, and it will, pause and greet it. No drama. No shame. Just presence.

Say the name.

Soften, if you can.

Then choose the response that

is more loving to you[2].

The next step of The Dissolve is where that awareness becomes movement.

It is where we learn to Soften It.

Mini Dissolve

Notice the next moment your invisible barrier speaks. Instead of arguing, simply name it. What shifts in your body when you do?

---

2   If that feels like it is off the table, then you are in the right place. Keep at it. You got this.

Chapter 3

Soften It

As you've seen, naming brings the invisible
barrier into your awareness. Softening
is how you begin to loosen it so it no
longer blocks your path to success.

Most people try to break an
invisible barrier with force.

That will not work.

Force reinforces it. Softening dissolves it.

Once you fully see the invisible barrier clearly,
your instinct is often to fight it or fix it or

outthink it. But the invisible barrier feeds
on tension. The more you push against it,
the more force it uses to stabilize itself.

So, we do the opposite.

We soften.

Letting Go

Softening is not weakness or avoidance
or quitting. It is precision removal. It
is how you stop fighting yourself.

Every client I guide through this
step asks the same question.

If I let go, won't everything fall apart?

This is the invisible barrier's favorite
strategy. It convinces you that your tension
is the glue holding your world together.

Sarah was convinced that rest could turn her
into someone sloppy and careless. I see this often
with clients, where they feel they must be "on"
all the time, both at work and at home. That is

a clear path straight to burnout and overwhelm. Jonah believed that his value came entirely from being seen, producing, and achieving. In his mind, the moment he stopped being visibly productive, people would forget about him and move on to someone else who was still in motion. If he kept the momentum going, then he mattered. But as I imagine you've experience before, we all run out of steam eventually and need to take breaks. It's those breaks that help us come back to work feeling refreshed and clear-headed so we can do our best work.

Maya feared that sharing unfinished ideas would make people think she didn't know what she was talking about. And similarly to Jonah, I used to believe that the moment I stopped working, people would think I wasn't valuable.

I stopped producing, my value would evaporate.

Softening does not dismantle your drive.

It refines it. It heals it. It frees it to expand.

Kai

Kai struggled most with the softening step.

He was intense, commanding, and protective.
Control was his love language. When we met,
he led a team of brilliant people who admired
him and feared disappointing him. He was not
trying to intimidate them. He genuinely thought
he was inspiring them toward excellence.

But beneath his strength was exhaustion.

"If I do not stay on top of everything,"
he told me, "It all unravels. I am
holding so much, all the time."

That was his invisible barrier, which he
would later name The General. The General
believed that power required pressure and
that leadership meant constant vigilance.

I asked Kai to imagine what would
happen if The General took a day off.

He froze.

"I do not know who I would be," he said.

Softening begins in a moment like this.
When you can sit with the discomfort
of not knowing what happens next.

When control loosens its grip and uncertainty
feels possible, even if it is uncomfortable. It is
the moment you stay instead of tightening.

Umbrellas in the Storm

Softening starts in the body long
before it reaches the mind.

When I work with clients, I often ask them
to pause mid-sentence and notice what
happens physically when they describe
their stuckness. They notice things like
tension in their shoulders and jaw, the way
their breathing feels forced or fast.

It is like watching someone grip an
umbrella harder in a heavy storm, convinced
that tension will stop the wind.

Most do not even realize it is raining.

So, I ask them to do something radical.

Unclench. Take a slow breath. Drop your
shoulders. Loosen your jaw. Let your
tongue fall from the roof of your mouth.

Not because breathing solves the
problem, but because it creates space
for a new possibility to appear.

Softening is an act of trust. Trust that the
world will not collapse if you stop bracing
against it. Trust that you can meet the
moment without tightening first.

Kai's Pause

Kai's first assignment was simple. *Say
less. Listen more. Hold the pause.*

In his next meeting, he sat back instead of leaning
forward. He noticed how quickly his body wanted
to jump in and take control. He could feel The
General pacing inside him, barking orders.

So, he did what The Dissolve teaches.
He named it, then softened.

He took a breath. He felt his feet on the ground. He paused. He stayed aware of what The General wanted him to do. He let the urge pass. He wrote notes in the margins of the agenda instead of speaking.

For the first time, his team filled the silence. They waited. They tested the space. Then, little by little, they stepped into it.

The room felt awkward. As if The General might burst in at any moment. No one knew what to do with this new version of Kai. But they found clarity and ownership that had not been possible before.

Afterward he told me, "It was so uncomfortable I wanted to crawl out of my skin. But then it started working."

This was progress!

When you first start softening, it can feel like you're losing something important: your control, your identity, your power, your edge. It feels like giving up what's been keeping you safe. But once you push through that discomfort, you realize you haven't lost anything real. You've actually freed yourself from something that was restricting you.

Softening often feels like loss right before it feels like liberation. It is clumsy before it is natural.

Kai was a novice, wobbling like a child riding a bike without training wheels for the first time.

And The General did not like that. Not one bit.

Sovereignty

Your nervous system cannot tell the difference between control and safety until you teach it. Then practice it. Then integrate it.

That is what this step is for.

You are teaching your system that softness is not surrender. Softness is sovereignty. It is you returning to yourself.

When Sarah softened, she expected nothing but disappointment. Instead she felt quiet. Anxious, but quiet.

When Jonah softened, he expected invisibility. Instead he found presence. He was nervous, but present.

When Maya softened, she expected misunderstanding. It hurt at first.

When Kai softened, he expected to lose power. Instead, he found connection. He felt awkward but connected.

Softening does not erase your edge. It removes the armor that restricts it.

Start Here

You can begin softening with four small moves.

1. **Notice tension.** Where in your body do you feel the alarm when you feel behind, judged, or inadequate?

2. **Name it.** Say the invisible barrier's name with gentleness. Haras, I see you. Clock Demon, I know. Curator, it is safe to share. General, there is no emergency here.

3. **Breathe once, fully.** Let your exhale be longer than your inhale. Drop your tongue to the bottom of your mouth.

4. **Do nothing for five seconds.** Let the silence or stillness exist without rushing to fill it. Let the discomfort be present.

This is softening.

It is microscopic and massive at the same time.

It is simple to access, and the more often you practice it, the more your system transforms.

Nourishment

Kai later said, "I used to think leadership meant holding everything together. Turns out, leadership is being at home in myself and letting everything else breathe."

That is the paradox of softening.

It feels like release and functions as stability.

People imagine softening is letting the garden die.

In truth, softening is the water and sunlight and nourishment that help it thrive.

Mini Dissolve

What part of you is afraid that softness means surrender?

What might happen if that part were allowed to experience something new?

Navigating the Uncomfortably Long Pause

Softening looks different for everyone,
but it always begins the same way. With a
pause that feels uncomfortably long.

That pause is sacred. It is the moment your
old wiring begins to unwind. It is the moment
you stop being manipulated by your invisible
barriers, notice the puppet strings, and
remember that you are not a puppet at all.

Kai once told me that silence used to feel
like a summons to act. In meetings, in
conversations, even at home, he filled every
gap with instruction or solution. It was not
arrogance. It was protection. The General
believed that control kept everyone safe.

After that first experiment, Kai began
using pauses as practice. Before replying
to a tense email. Before making a decision.
Before entering a conversation. He stopped
just long enough to feel his heartbeat.

At first it felt like standing awkwardly in a
spotlight. Then, slowly, it began to feel like clarity.

The General still paced inside him, but Kai no longer mistook the pacing for orders to act.

With practice, he could hold silence for a few heartbeats, then a minute, then longer.

Sarah

Sarah's softening was quieter and just as brave. She started with five minutes of unstructured time in the morning. No lists. No optimized routines. No productive reading. Just coffee and awareness.

At first, Haras hated it. Which meant Sarah hated it.

The voice in her head insisted, You are wasting time. You should be doing something useful.

She kept unconsciously reaching for her planner, catching herself, setting it down, and returning to stillness.

She stayed with it.

One morning she noticed sunlight flickering through the blinds and wondered, *When did I stop seeing this?*

That was her first real dissolve. Not in a coaching session. Not on a retreat. But in a quiet kitchen filled with morning light.

Softening often begins in the mundane. It is not a grand epiphany. It is a recalibration. Your relationship to the world shifts, and that shift is everything.

You remember that inspiration used to be available to you in the everyday. Your invisible barrier simply kept you from noticing it.

Jonah

Softening does not mean you stop caring. It means you stop gripping care so tightly that you choke the life out of it.

Jonah struggled with that distinction. When he first tried slowing down, he assumed it meant laziness. If I do not push, nothing moves, he said.

So we tested it. One week. No pushing on one project he chose. He could still work, but without urgency.

By day two he was unraveling. On the morning
of day three, we spoke briefly, and he realized
something profound. His creativity did not
disappear when he slowed down. It deepened.

Still uncomfortable. Still confronting. But
he sensed there was treasure on the other
side of the softness, if he could tolerate the
discomfort long enough to reach it.

Softening happens in layers. First, he softened
toward The Clock Demon. Then toward
the discomfort of ignoring its orders.

After two weeks, he began writing again,
not for deadlines but for pleasure. The Clock
Demon still told him, "You are falling behind,"
but it no longer dictated his choices.

Softness had not erased his fire. It had refined
it. It had opened a creative channel that could
not breathe when he was pushing all the time.

Maya

Softening for Maya happened in the space
before motion. Her invisible barrier was not
urgency or over-responsibility. It was retreat.

When Maya felt misunderstood or overwhelmed,
she did not push harder like Jonah. She
disappeared. Not physically. But mentally.
She slipped into the cathedral of her mind
where everything was ordered and safe.

Softening meant doing the opposite
of what she had practiced for decades.
It meant staying in the room.

Her experiment was small and almost invisible
from the outside. Before withdrawing in a
conversation, before her attention drifted
inward, before her eyes softened into distance,
she gave herself a cue. *Feel your feet.*

The first time she tried it, she said
it felt like stepping onto a stage she
never intended to walk onto.

Everything in her wanted to retreat into analysis, where she felt capable and protected. But she stayed. Just for a breath. Then two.

One afternoon during a team discussion, she felt the old pattern rise. The sense that she was talking too long or boring people. She could already feel herself pulling away, the way a tide pulls sand from under your feet.

Instead of disappearing, she paused.

She inhaled. Exhaled.

And asked, "Is this landing for you?"

It was small. But saying those words created a bridge where a wall normally went up.

Later she told me that moment scared her more than any presentation she had ever given. Not because the stakes were high. But because she stayed present when her instinct was to vanish.

That was her softening. Not becoming louder. Not forcing confidence. Not performing.

Just staying long enough to feel the connection
she always assumed she was losing.

Over time, those pauses felt less like hanging
over the edge of a cliff and more like resting
points. She learned she did not need to shrink
her brilliance to avoid disconnection. She just
needed her awareness in the room with her
body instead of leaving her body behind.

Softening did not make her less precise
or thoughtful or deep. It made her
accessible. To others and to herself.

And as she practiced, something unexpected
happened. Her ideas stopped feeling fragile.
Staying present did not drain her. It grounded her.

Softness became the doorway through
which she could share the full shape of
her mind without losing herself in it.

Force is Expensive

There is a myth that force is the only way
forward. That intensity equals impact. But force

is expensive. It drains your nervous system. It erodes relationships. It narrows your vision.

The biggest lie we learned is that force gives us new results. It does not. Force guarantees repeated results and diminishing returns.

Softness expands capacity.

When you soften, you gain access to nuance, intuition, timing, and real presence. You stop hammering at problems and begin listening to what they actually need.

This is why The Dissolve does not dismantle ambition. It upgrades it. Softened ambition is powerful because it is sustainable. It does not crash. It does not burn. It breathes.

It expands without limits.

Magnetic

I learned this the hard way.

Early in my career, I mistook tension for commitment. If I was not slightly anxious,

I assumed I was not trying hard enough. My body lived in a constant low-grade sprint.

I learned early in my athletic career that feeling anxious and amped up before a race was a sign that I was about to get a personal record. Discomfort, anxiety, and wasted energy was a sign that I cared and was about to succeed.

I applied that learning to my early career and it looked like narrowing my focus on an email thinking that energy draining laser focus on those two paragraphs would somehow signal to the recipient that I was here to *crush it*. That was both ineffective at communicating my desire to achieve and completely exhausting. I applied that laser like focus to everything, all day, and without rest.

When I began practicing The Dissolve on myself, the hardest part was not admitting I was tired. It was admitting I was scared. Scared that if I softened, I would stop mattering. Scared that ease would make me irrelevant.

But the opposite happened. When I stopped muscling every outcome, my work began to flow. Clients found me instead of me chasing them. Ideas that used to take weeks arrived in days.

Softening did not make me smaller.
It made me magnetic.

Early in my career I used to do a lot of planning
before I went to a networking event because I
knew having the right conversation with the
right person would open up opportunities.
That looked like scouring the attendee list,
making a spreadsheet of their name, bio, and
thinking of questions I could ask them when
I orchestrated a conversation with them. It
took a lot of work and was exhausting. This
is the Caffeinated Manager invisible barrier
that you'll read more about in a few pages.

Now when I go to networking events, I take a
softer approach that not only feels better but is
1000x more effective. I practice feeling the way
the people I want to speak with will feel when they
meet me and enjoy our conversation. I remind
myself to feel that multiple times a day for the
days and weeks leading up to the event. When I
get to the event, I bring up that practiced feeling,
with no expectation of the outcome. The result of
this is that I have lovely conversations in a relaxed
way and more often than not, we follow up in
meaningful ways that are mutually beneficial.

Argue

If you are trying this for the first time, expect
resistance. The invisible barrier will argue.
It will warn you that you are slipping, that
you are undisciplined, that you are betraying
your potential, or that you will get hurt.

That is its job.

When it happens, notice it.

Name it.

Breathe.

Stay soft.

You are teaching your system that safety and
stillness can coexist. Once it learns that, you will
never need to force your way forward again.

Mini Dissolve

Pause for ten seconds. Notice where in your body
you feel tense. Where do you feel like you're still
needing to grip tightly to control? What changes
when you let it melt by one degree?

Micro Softening

The hardest part about softening is that no one can see it from the outside. It does not photograph well. It does not announce itself. There is no applause when you unclench your jaw or take one slow breath instead of firing back an email.

But this is where real change happens. Internally, with micro-softening.

Every micro-softening trains your system in a new rhythm. You start replacing the familiar pulse of do, fix, prove with a quieter one: notice, allow, create.

This is how The Dissolve fuels your new life.

Leading from a Place of Calm Instead of Fear

Kai once told me, "I always thought calm, quiet people did not care as much."

He was not alone. In high-stakes spaces, intensity and volume are often mistaken

for commitment. We reward urgency. We
glorify the grind. We idolize the bold.

But calm is not indifference. It is mastery.

When Kai practiced softening in leadership
and stayed with it through the discomfort, his
influence deepened. Instead of commanding
compliance, he invited collaboration. The
shift was subtle enough that his team
could not name it, but they felt it. A few
even asked if he was feeling all right.

Meetings became shorter and more effective.
His presence felt magnetic instead of militant.

Later he said, "I used to think I was leading by
strength. Turns out, I was leading by fear."

That is what The Dissolve reveals.
Fear disguised as excellence.

A terrified monarch hiding behind high
castle walls, a moat, and guards at the
gate is not a world-class leader.

Recognizing the True Problem Under What You *Think* Is the Problem

Softening exposes truth.

When Sarah loosened her grip on constant self-correction, she discovered she was not a perfectionist. She was an idealist. Her standards were never the problem. Her rigidity was.

When she released the need to critique everything she touched, her integrity did not vanish. It expanded. Her work remained precise, but now it carried energy that fueled creativity instead of draining it.

She told me, "I thought relaxing my grip would make everything sloppy. It did not. It made everything human."

Exactly. Humanity is the ingredient perfectionism tries to hide from.

Softness Allows for Connection

Maya's softening was quiet and profound. Once she stopped polishing every idea

to death, she realized how lonely her
brilliance had become. The Curator had
promised safety but delivered isolation.

When she began sharing ideas mid-formation,
messy and alive, something remarkable happened.
People leaned in. Collaboration replaced
curation. Connection replaced over-editing.

She said, "Softening feels like letting people
touch what I love without breaking it."

That is the whole point.

Softness makes connection possible.
And it allows you to trust more.

Presence

Softening is not a destination. It is a mode
of travel. Once you learn it, you can bring
it anywhere. In conversation. In creative
work. In conflict. In leadership.

I use it every day.

Before a big event, when the old proving energy starts humming, I pause. I notice where my body activates and what my instincts are telling me to do. I exhale once, fully. Then I remind myself that pressure does not make me powerful. Presence does.

That is my Dissolve.

I do not silence the drive. I Name it and Soften it until that old instinct melts back into presence.

Ease

Here is what I know after walking thousands of people through this. If you get good at softening, life rushes in to meet you.

Opportunities that once felt forced begin to unfold. Relationships begin to breathe. You stop negotiating every moment for worth.

Softening is not easy. But it leads you to ease.

Ease is where clarity lives.

If you are realizing that softening is something
you want to practice, not just understand,
you are not alone. This is the core of the work
I do with people. Learning how to stay soft
without losing your edge. Learning how to
lead from presence instead of pressure.

Start practicing freedom right
now, with your own body.

Take one more breath.

Unclench your jaw.

Lower your shoulders.

Soften your eyes.

Allow your nervous system to experience freedom.

Mini Dissolve

Think of one area where you have been gripping control. What would it look like to lead that same situation from softness instead of force?

Chapter 4

Sashay Through It

By the time you reach the Sashay step in this process, you have already done two brave things.

You have Named It—brought the invisible barrier into form.

You have Softened It—and taught your body it can sit with that barrier without bracing.

Sashay is what happens next.

Not when you go crush it in the world.

Not when you land the promotion or nail the talk.

Sashay is the in-between.

It is where you rehearse being your
future self while the track is closed.

The Track Is Closed

Formula 1 race drivers often compete on
new courses through tight European cities
and only get a limited number of training
laps. During those laps, they are going all
out, turning corners at impossible speeds,
feeling every vibration in their bodies.

Later, when the track is closed and the cars
are parked, they keep driving laps anyway.

They sit still.

They put on an eye mask.

They do not eat. They do not move.

They turn down the volume on
four of their five senses.

And they listen to the audio from their practice laps. The sound of their own engines flying through those same corners and straightaways.

They are teaching their bodies
to thrive on that track.

By the time race day comes, it is not unknown anymore. It is familiar because their nervous system has already been there.

They have rehearsed the version of themselves that feels safe, open, and thriving on the new course.

That is what Sashay is.

It is you, eyes closed and track closed, rehearsing how it feels to live as the person you are becoming before you are asked to do it at full speed in front of everyone.

Turning Down Who You Have Been

When you turn down the volume on your five senses, you temporarily disconnect

from the environment that constantly
reminds you who you have been:

- The room you always hustle in
- The laptop where your overwork lives
- The phone that carries your obligations
- The faces and places that cue your old
  reactions

Those signals pull you back into
your familiar identity.

When you turn the volume down on those inputs,
your eyes closed, your body still, nothing to
fix, you give your system a chance to rehearse
who you are becoming instead. Just like the
Formula 1 drivers learn who they are when
they are comfortable on the new course.

You are not escaping reality. You
are rehearsing a new one.

In Sashay, you take the invisible
barrier you have named and softened
and begin to build a relationship with
Future You on the other side of it.

You design that self.

You practice that self.

You normalize that self.

So that later, when the same old triggers
show up, your body does not panic. It
recognizes the moment and thinks: "Oh,
we have been here. This is us now."

The Night Before the Talk

I have been speaking in front of people
since I was in third grade. I fell in love with
it the first time I stepped up to a mic.

But for most of my life, my
internal process was brutal.

I would write talks and then force myself to
memorize them in a tight, punishing way. Late
nights. Clenched jaw. Running lines until my
eyes blurred. I measured my worth in perfect
timing, flawless slides, and hitting every cue.

It worked, in the sense that I performed well.

But the invisible barrier behind it was vicious.

I called it The Caffeinated Manager.

Not long ago, I had the chance to learn a new body
of material from a globally renowned presenter.
I had less than a day to absorb it, and then I was
scheduled to deliver his content back to him, in
person, in front of about a hundred people.

High stakes. Little time. Classic
setup for my old pattern.

Weeks before I even flew to the
venue, I started Sashaying.

I mentally rehearsed learning new material
from calm instead of from panic. I pictured
myself sitting in the room, heart open, mind
present, body grounded. I felt what it would
be like to say, "I belong here," and mean it.

I was not repeating lines. I was
rehearsing a state of being.

In my meditations, with my eyes closed and
the volume of my everyday life turned down,
I practiced being the version of me who could
learn quickly from love, calm, and openness
instead of fear. I sat with the old urge to grind

myself into the ground and stayed with the future
self who did not need cruelty to be excellent.

By the time I reached the event, that version
of me was not a fantasy anymore. My
nervous system had already met her.

The night before the talk, I felt The Caffeinated
Manager try to reassert itself. I could feel
the urge to stay up all night, to force myself
into perfect-performance-machine-mode,
to rehearse until my body was shaking.

For two hours, the temptation was loud.

Every time I caught it, I paused my preparations
and softened. I remembered who I had
already practiced becoming, the person who
learns from a place of calm, openness, and
love, not from force and stress. The one who
trusts presence more than punishment.

The next day, just before I walked on
stage to deliver his material back to
him, my body did what bodies do.

My heart pounded. My gut tightened. I suddenly
felt like I needed to bolt to the bathroom, just

like pre-race jitters from my distance-running days. That fear loop fired, fast and automatic, as it always does. The Caffeinated Manager snapped to attention. There is no version of transformation where that loop disappears.

The difference now was that I did not mistake it for a problem or mindlessly obey The Caffeinated Manager's instructions.

I stayed in my chair. I attended to the feeling. I reminded myself, "This is the moment you rehearsed for. This is where you show yourself who you have already become."

When I stood up to speak, I did not deliver the talk I had written word for word. I did not even deliver the talk I had rehearsed the night before. I delivered the talk my body had been practicing in meditation for weeks: embodied, present, clear, rooted, and free. I got the whole idea across, and the content landed with clarity. But more than that, I landed in a new, unpredictable experience.

The globally renowned presenter responded very enthusiastically. I was completely unprepared for how positive and affirming his response was.

Afterward, one of the trainers pulled me aside and said, "In ten years, I have never seen him respond like that."

That was not luck. That was Sashay.

Not because I forced myself to rise to the occasion, but because I had quietly rehearsed being that version of me so many times that, when the lights came up, my system stepped into it like a well-worn track and trusted the unknown, uncontrolled, unpredictable experience.

That is what The Dissolve does. It expands what is possible in ways you could never have planned.

What Sashay Does in Your Brain and Body

Here is the simplest way I know to say it:
- First you have an idea of who you are becoming.
- Then, in meditation, you give yourself an experience of being that person.

Idea plus experience enriches the neural networks in your neocortex. The new self stops being theoretical and starts becoming wired and real.

Repetition stabilizes those patterns.

You are gently retraining your fear loop. The fast, automatic response that screams, "Unknown, danger," will still fire. But over time, it starts to meet the future as something familiar.

Not because you shut off fear. But because your system has a new reference point: "This is not unknown anymore. We have been here. We belong. We can thrive here." Your nervous system stops treating your expansion as a threat and starts recognizing it as normal, safe, and known.

That is the job of Sashay: To make your future self feel less like a stretch and more like home.

The Sashay Protocol

Here is how you can start Sashaying on purpose. You do not have to get it perfect. In fact, perfection is the opposite of what this step is for. Perfect is predictable, and predictable is just more of the same, is it not?

1. Choose the Future You Are Rehearsing

Pick one specific way of being on the other side of your invisible barrier. For example:

- For Sarah: Her choice was to be present and non-reactive with a full inbox. To remember that she didn't need to respond to everyone immediately.
- For Jonah: He wanted to be able to sit in a meeting and not need to grab onto every loose task.
- For Maya: She could share her ideas and stay in the room when the room went quiet.
- For Kai: He wanted to lead a high-stakes conversation without force.

Do not try to rehearse your entire life. Start with one scene, one way of being, or one room you want to inhabit differently.

2. Turn Down the Volume on Who You Have Been

Find a quiet place. Sit or lie down and close your eyes.

You are not trying to empty your mind.
You are turning down the sensory
inputs that keep reminding you:

This is your office. This is your inbox. This
is the room where you always brace.

Let the external world dim a little. This is
where you will keep running practice laps,
even though the new course is closed.

3. Step Into Your Future Self

Now use your brilliant brain to embody the
situation you chose, from the perspective of the
you who has already dissolved this barrier.

Where are you? Who is with you? What are you
doing with your hands, your shoulders, your eyes?

Most importantly: How does it feel in your
body to be that person? Do not rush. Let
yourself feel it as fully as you can. Calm, clear,
grounded, curious, or whatever emotions fit.

4. Let Your Body Learn It

Stay with the sensation, even if your mind tries to label it as fake or pretend. You are teaching your system, "This is me now, and this is what normal can feel like."

The longer you can rest there, the more familiar it becomes. There is no strain, no grading yourself. Just repetition of ease.

5. Repeat Until It Feels Less Impressive and More Obvious

You will know Sashay is working when your future self stops feeling like a peak moment and starts feeling strangely unremarkable. Natural. Obvious.

That is the point.

You are not trying to become a superhero. You are becoming someone your nervous system trusts you to be when the stakes are high.

If you want support, you can get the same meditations I use with my clients when they begin the Sashay step at thedissolve.me.

Sarah's Sashay

You met Sarah when her days were ruled by
Haras, the inner auditor who never let her rest.
Her first softening was tiny. Five minutes alone
in the morning with coffee and no productivity.
Just light through the blinds, breath, and being.

At first, that was all she could handle.
But over time, she began to extend that
window. Ten minutes. Fifteen. Some days
she missed it entirely. Old Sarah would
have turned that into another failure.

New Sarah practiced grace.

In Sashay, she used those moments as a
track-closed rehearsal space. She imagined
herself in the middle of a busy week, staying
present and gentle instead of rigid and reactive.
She pictured herself in conversations with
people she loved, not rehearsing arguments
in her head, but actually listening.

She mentally rehearsed being the version
of herself who could sit at the dinner table
or in a team meeting without scanning
for everything that was wrong.

In Sashay, she could look at her inbox and stay calm and clear-headed instead of seeing it as a mountain of proof that she was failing.

Over time, her system learned that this was not laziness. It was leadership. The payoff showed up in her business. Because she no longer needed to carry everything herself to prove her goodness, she began to delegate, collaborate, and release her grip on inbox zero.

She became less brittle and more effective. Integrity without self-punishment.

That is Sashay.

Jonah's Sashay

Jonah had already named an invisible barrier: The Clock Demon. But as we worked, another barrier revealed itself.

We called it The Gilded Dustpan.

Jonah had a gift. He could spot tiny undone tasks, loose ends, messy corners, and scoop them up fast. He had been rewarded his whole life for this.

The dustpan was gilded because he had learned it was a kind of trophy. Praise and external validation had coated it in gold. But it was heavy.

Every time someone dropped a task in a meeting, Jonah grabbed it before it hit the floor. He was drowning in extra work he had convinced himself only he could do, while quietly resenting that no one else stepped up.

In Sashay, he began rehearsing something radical: Letting the dust sit.

Eyes closed, track closed, he pictured himself in a real meeting. Someone suggested a new project. Normally, his hand would shoot up automatically.

Instead, in his mental rehearsal, he stayed still. He let the suggestion hang in the air. He felt the urge to volunteer rise like a wave, and he practiced not riding it.

He imagined himself asking clarifying questions instead: "What outcome matters most here? Who is best positioned to own this?"

He rehearsed feeling competent and valuable without being the one who swept up every responsibility. So when the moment finally came, in a high-stakes room with a mentor two layers above him, his body already knew what to do.

A complex, burdensome task was floated. Everyone subconsciously turned toward Jonah.

The old impulse surged. The Gilded Dustpan rattled.

But he stayed in his chair. He breathed. He asked questions instead of volunteering.

His mentor later told him, "That was the most strategic I have ever seen you in a meeting."

That is Sashay.

Maya's Sashay

Maya had named The Curator, the careful inner keeper who polished every idea behind glass. But she discovered another barrier hiding beneath it.

She called it Shouting Into The Void.

Whenever she shared something complex or deeply thought through, she watched people's faces like her life depended on it. If they frowned, glanced away, or looked confused, she took it as a verdict: No one gets me. I should retreat. I should stop sharing.

In Sashay, she began rehearsing a different story.

Eyes closed, she pictured herself in a real conversation, sharing an idea that mattered, watching someone's attention waver.

Old Maya would have shut down or over-explained. Future Maya, her Sashay self, did something else.

She paused. She stayed present. She asked some questions.

"What is landing for you so far?" she said. "What feels clear? What feels muddy?"

She imagined feeling curious instead of wounded. Collaborative instead of dismissed.

She rehearsed dozens of these conversations in meditation. She experienced the same

sensation in her chest and the same flicker
of fear, but with a new response.

So, when it happened in real life, when a senior
colleague's eyes glazed over halfway through her
explanation, her body recognized the moment.

She did not retreat. She smiled, paused, and said,
"Okay, I can feel I have gone detailed. What are
you most interested in understanding here?"

The colleague leaned back in, re-engaged,
and together they co-shaped a version of her
idea that landed across the whole team.

That is Sashay.

Kai's Sashay

Kai leads with power. For years, his invisible
barrier, The General, kept him and his
company alive by gripping control.

As the company grew, Kai started seeing a future
version of himself that his current nervous
system did not yet know how to be. A leader

in bigger boardrooms, with bigger investors,
higher stakes, and more visible consequences.

In Sashay, he closed his eyes and put
himself there.

Board table. High-stakes presentation.
Faces that did not smile easily. In his
inner rehearsal, he was not armored.

He was clear. Grounded. Listening. Collaborative.

He practiced staying at the head of the table
without dominating it. He imagined asking
questions instead of issuing orders. He
rehearsed hearing hard feedback without
flaring into defensiveness or shutdown.

Again and again, behind closed eyes, he
ran laps around that future boardroom.

So, when the day came and he walked into the
real thing, bigger investors, more serious board,
real risk on the line, his body was not shocked.

The General flared, of course. The old protector
always does. But Kai recognized the sensation

and remembered the leader he had already
practiced being. He found his breath.

He stayed open. He led the room without force.

Afterward, one of the board members said,
"You look like you are already running
the next version of this company."

That is Sashay.

Sashay Is Not About Crushing It

Sashay is not about hyping yourself up to
perform as your future self, as if you were
learning to portray a character on a stage.

It is about spending enough time with that
version of you that, when life asks you to show
up differently, your body does not argue.

Sashay is about enjoying the process of
becoming Future You. Enjoyment is a healing
salve for the toll your invisible barriers
have taken on you and the toll that leads
so many high achievers to burnout.

You will still feel the old responses. The urge to overwork. The twitch to volunteer. The pull to retreat. The need to command. The instant fear loop will still fire without giving you a chance to think. That is how your system works.

But now, when it does, you have a deeper reference point:

"I know who I am becoming, and I have met Future Me. I have learned their rhythm. This is my track now."

That is what it means to Sashay Through It.

Mini Dissolve, Sashay Edition

Close your eyes. Picture one specific moment in your near future where your old pattern always takes over. For thirty seconds, rehearse being the version of you who moves through that moment with ease, presence, and softness.

Let yourself enjoy this sensation.
Enjoy enjoying it.

What would it feel like if that version of you was not extraordinary, but normal?

Chapter 5

Dissolving In Real Time

By now, you have learned to Name It,
Soften It, and Sashay Through It.

But the real power of The Dissolve is not in using
those steps once. It is in using them over and over,
in real time, when life inevitably gets loud again.

Because the truth is, you never stop hitting
barriers. You just stop mistaking them for failure.

Not Zen

The people who integrate this work do not
live in a perpetual state of Zen. They still get
triggered. They still overcommit. They still
feel the invisible barrier hum on bad days.

The difference is that they recognize
it much more quickly.

That is what dissolving in real time looks like.

Awareness on the fly. Adjustment without shame.

When you can feel the resistance rising,
name it, soften your stance, and move
through, all in one breath, you are no
longer just practicing The Dissolve.

You are The Dissolve.

In every space where I teach this work, one
on one, with executive teams, and inside The
Dissolve Year, we practice exactly this. We
take live pressure and turn it into real time
dissolves until your system knows the way
back without you having to think about it.

Checking In as a Way to Dissolve

Jonah learned to dissolve on the go.

He was in the middle of a product launch
when the Clock Demon started hissing about
lost time. Deadlines, analytics, comparisons,
all the old noise came rushing back.

But instead of drowning in urgency, he paused,
closed his laptop, and went for a walk.

He did not check out. He checked in.

By the time he returned, his brain had
quicted. He saw what actually mattered,
trimmed the busywork, and launched with
half the stress and double the clarity.

He said later, "The Demon is still around, but
he is quieter. It is like he knows I am listening
and does not get in my face so much anymore."

That is the subtle grace of real time dissolving. The
invisible barrier does not vanish. It transforms
into guidance and helps you see what you have
been missing while you were in overdrive.

This is where your invisible barriers
become a map to the treasure you seek.

Presence as a Way to Dissolve

Sarah's dissolves were quieter.

She caught Haras saying during her son's piano
recital, "You should be answering emails."

Old Sarah would have believed it. She
would have slipped into the guilt loop, half
listening to the music and half drafting
imaginary replies in her head.

This time, she smiled. She felt her
breath. She stayed present.

That is how The Dissolve shows up once
it is in your body. It becomes instinct.

It is not just a process anymore.

It is a posture.

Pivot Before Panic

Softening in motion does not mean you stop caring or striving. It means you learn to pivot before panicking. You sense the barrier forming and, instead of running headfirst into it, you flow sideways through the gap.

It is what jazz musicians do. They improvise around dissonance until it becomes melody. That is dissolving in real time. Turning tension into tempo.

Pressure Rising

The next time you feel the pressure rising, emails stacking, deadlines tightening, old patterns whispering, do not reach for control.

Reach for awareness.

Pause for one breath. Name the invisible barrier by name.

Soften your shoulders, your eyes, the tone of your voice, the tone of your muscles.

Then move one inch in the direction of freedom.

That is the entire method condensed into a single heartbeat. And if that is all you ever practice, it will still change everything.

Mini Dissolve

When the pressure hits next, catch it.

Name it.

Soften it.

Move one inch forward.

Notice how the barrier shifts when you do.

Responding in Real Time

Real-time dissolving is where
theory becomes instinct.

It is not about doing the steps perfectly. It is
about remembering you have steps at all.

Before The Dissolve, most people's nervous
systems are built on patterns of overdrive,
shutdown, proving, hiding, or perfecting. Fight
harder. Freeze longer. Get out of there. Those
were the only options the system knew.

Naming, softening, and sashaying
introduce something entirely new in
high-stakes moments: responsiveness.

You are not a victim of the moment and you
are not trying to dominate the moment.

You are in dialogue with it.

Expansion

Maya described dissolving in real time as "learning to catch the spin before it becomes a storm."

She was on a panel when a fellow expert challenged her mid-sentence.

The Curator snapped to attention. She felt her chest tighten. Racing thoughts. The familiar urge to retreat behind intellect. That old pattern had kept her safe for decades.

But instead of disappearing into analysis, she breathed.

She smiled and said, "That is an interesting angle. Let's explore it."

The room relaxed. The tension dissolved. Later she told me, "It felt like I had all the space in the world."

That is what dissolving in real time does. It expands time. When you stop reacting, reality slows down and you see options panic has been hiding from you. This is where

you finally see the treasure your invisible
barriers kept you too distracted to notice.

Holding Space Without Pressure

Kai learned this in conflict.

Old Kai would enter a disagreement like a
storm. Command first. Understand later.
That was The General's doctrine for survival.
But The General had been retrained.

During a critical negotiation, his team
was split on strategy. The familiar surge
hit. The urge to assert control. His hands
tightened on the edge of the table.

Instead of launching into directives,
he paused. He leaned back and said,
"Tell me what I am not seeing."

The room exhaled.

He did not lose authority. He gained influence.

Afterward he told me, "I realized leadership
isn't holding the line. It is holding the space."

That is dissolving in real time.

Presence without pressure. Power without force.

Pausing Again and Again Throughout the Day

Sarah's real-time dissolves appeared in micro-moments: at stoplights, before calls, during dinner.

She used to believe peace was circumstantial.
Something she could only feel when the
inbox was empty or the house was quiet.

Now she found it inside the mess,
in the middle of motion.

Her practice was simple: treat pauses as practice.
A red light became a breath. A delay became
a dissolve. A mistake became a teacher.

She told me, "I do not wait for the world to
calm down anymore. I carry calm with me."
That is mastery. Not control. Consistency.

Real-Time Dissolving

The more you practice dissolving in real
time, the more your nervous system learns
that safety is internal, not situational. You
stop outsourcing peace to perfect conditions.
You begin generating it from within.

These are the moments when everything changes,
because now you can create, lead, and love from a
place that does not require external permission.

Peace allows you to expand beyond the limits
your invisible barriers had you trapped behind.

Unexpected and Delightful Results

One of my favorite dissolves did not happen
in a boardroom or during a keynote.

It happened on a treadmill.

Years ago, I was a Division I distance
runner. I had raced countless times inside
my invisible barriers. Driven. Disciplined.
Quietly punishing myself for every split.

Two years ago, I wondered if I could run
a timed mile in under seven minutes
again. I trained for nine months. But
differently this time. I sashayed into it.

I ran because it felt good, not because
I needed to prove anything.

I did it. First sub-seven mile in thirty-five years.
Sweet, proud, steady. The payoff from nine
months of dissolving and enjoying the process.

Then a year passed. Injuries. Setbacks.
Life. I had not trained the same way. Old
Me would have braced for disappointment.
Analyzed. Justified. Forced. But that day at
the gym, I decided to dissolve in real time.

Standing on the treadmill, one sentence arrived
with absolute clarity: "I am the version of myself
who thinks it is really fun to run super fast."

Instead of trying harder or forcing
anything, I chose. I simply chose.

Then something unexpected happened. A warm
glow squeezed through my whole body. Soft.

Expansive. Familiar in a way I could not explain.
It felt like the future version of me arriving early.

I smiled. Two seconds later, the coach told
us to begin. I punched in the speed that
should get me under seven minutes. I started
running. It felt effortless. So effortless I
thought I had typed the wrong speed.

I looked down. It was right. My
whole system had agreed.

I crossed the line at 6:56, smiling the entire
way. That was not about fitness. Or discipline.
Or performance. It was my nervous system
learning, in real time, "This is who we are now."

That is dissolving.

The moment the warm glow arrived,
the outcome was already irrelevant.

My identity had changed first.

Tiny Corrections

Real-time dissolving is not glamorous. It is a
thousand small course corrections that create
a new life. When you live this way, stuckness
becomes information rather than indictment.
Each invisible barrier becomes a teacher.

You start trusting your own capacity
to return. That is freedom.

Not the absence of friction, but the certainty
that you can move with it. Real-time dissolving
is when you become the student of your invisible
barriers so they can finally stop holding you back.

Mini Dissolve

When something small goes wrong today, do not
fix it immediately.

Name the discomfort.

Soften your response.

Move with grace.

See what opens when you do.

Reprogramming Your Entire System

Dissolving in real time is the proof that
your system has been reprogrammed. You
stop chasing balance and start creating
rhythm. And that rhythm does not disappear
when life gets messy. It gets louder.

That is the paradox. The more chaotic things
become, the more obvious your calm becomes.

Realizing Your Contributions
Are Enough

Maya's real-time dissolves began slipping into
her work almost without her noticing. The
Curator had once insisted that every idea be
flawless before it ever saw daylight. But as she
practiced staying present instead of retreating,
she experimented with something radical
for her: sharing ideas at eighty percent.

She posted things that were unfinished,
imperfect, honest. And the world did not
collapse. In fact, she felt herself opening.

She told me, "Every time I share something unfinished, I feel a little more alive." That is the truth of real-time dissolving. Life does not reward polish. Life rewards presence.

What If Slowing Down Could Feel Safe Again?

Jonah's dissolves emerged in the one place his invisible barriers used to dominate: pace. For most of his career, the Clock Demon set the tempo. Every task felt like a sprint. Every meeting felt timed. Every quiet moment became an opportunity to fall behind.

Slowing down felt like danger. Pausing felt like irresponsibility. His real-time dissolve began with one simple sentence he practiced in meetings:

"You do not need to grab the Gilded Dustpan."

The first time he tried it, he told me it felt like holding his breath underwater. But he stayed. He let the suggestion of a task hang in the air instead of sweeping it up. He let others step forward. He waited long enough to notice the old instinct fire and soften instead of obey it.

One afternoon, he caught himself listening instead of leaping. He felt the urge to over function rise. And dissolve.

He stayed in the pocket of the moment instead of racing ahead of it.

Later he said, "I didn't slow down. I just stopped speeding through my life."

That is dissolving in real time. A new rhythm emerging where urgency used to live.

Choose Awareness

You will know you are dissolving in real time when feedback stops landing like threat and silence stops landing like judgment. When you can pause mid-sentence, mid-email, or mid-thought and choose awareness instead of autopilot.

That micro-moment is where growth happens. It is the breath between stimulus and response.

It is the space where you move through what used to distract you automatically. Transformation rarely happens in the breakthrough. Transformation happens in the breath.

Integration

When I lead people through this work in groups, I remind them of one truth: You do not graduate from The Dissolve. You integrate it.

It becomes the way you walk, the way you communicate, the way you decide, the way you relate. You stop trying to get through challenges and start dancing with them. That is what Sarah meant when she said, "I still get triggered, but now I dissolve instead of detonate." That is what Jonah meant when he said, "I stopped waiting for permission to rest."

And it is what I mean when I tell clients that The Dissolve does not fix you. It frees you.

Remember

If you have made it this far, you already know the difference between motion and momentum.

Between pressure and presence.

The only practice left is remembering.

Remember to Name It when resistance rises.
Remember to Soften before you strategize.

Remember to move with grace instead of force. And when you forget, because you will, remember that you know how to return.

That is when The Dissolve becomes alive in you.

Mini Dissolve

When the next wave of chaos hits, do not brace.

Breathe.

Let the world move and stay in rhythm with
yourself.

Remember who you are becoming.

That is dissolving in real time.

Conclusion

Creation Without Limits

The moment you learn to dissolve in real time,
you stop chasing peace and start creating it.

Everything begins to change. Your work. Your
relationships. Your leadership. Your art.

Because when you are no longer driven by fear or
proof, the full force of your creativity comes online.

This is the promise of The Dissolve:
Not a life without barriers, but a life
where barriers become doorways.

Stop Fighting

Early in my life, I learned that who I was
could be dangerous, confusing, or too much. I
practiced that belief for forty years. It became
so automatic I nearly forgot it was learned.

Through The Dissolve, I softened those
patterns. I named the invisible barriers they
created, including The Over Crusher and
The Caffeinated Manager, then softened
and sashayed through each one.

Even now, when I encounter people or situations
that imply I am wrong, broken, or threatening,
the old loop fires fast. It rises instantly in my
throat, ready to catapult me into fight.

But now I dissolve it in real time. I feel
the fear loop. I attend to it internally.

I soften. I breathe. And I remind it: We are safe.
We are whole. We belong everywhere we go.

The results are dramatically different from the
previous forty years of my life. Before, I would
shout, posture, fight, dominate. I learned to
be so big that nothing could threaten me.

Now, I stay present. I stay grounded.
I listen. I ask questions. I learn. We find
understanding. We grow together. This is the
power of dissolving in real time. Situations
that once took me out are now places where
I see dramatically different outcomes.

Where would *you* like to experience that?

Stop the Patterns

Months after our last session, Sarah wrote to
me, "I don't think I've changed. I think I've
just stopped fighting who I already was."

That is it. That is The Dissolve in a single sentence.

Jonah calls it "operating at my natural speed."

Kai calls it "leading without armor."

Maya calls it "thinking out loud."

Different words. Same truth. Freedom is not
found outside the invisible barrier. Freedom
is found in your relationship with it.

You are already free. Your invisible barriers simply distracted you from that truth. When you believe, at your core, that who you are is GOOD, you move beyond the very barrier you designed to protect you.

Stuck

Here is what I want you to remember:
you will get stuck again.

You will tighten.

You will react.

You will brace, push, or spiral.

And when that happens, remember:
you already know the way back.

Name it. Soften it. Sashay right through it.
Every dissolve expands your range. Every
moment of grace returns you to yourself.
This is not self-help. This is self-return.

Presence

The world does not need more perfect people.
It needs more present ones. People who can
stay soft in chaos. Move through resistance
with rhythm. Lead with unarmored power.

You are one of them now.

You Are Dissolving

So, take one last breath with me. Inhale
possibility. Exhale pressure.

You are not behind. You are not broken. You are
dissolving, in real time, into your next becoming.

That is creation without limits.

That is The Dissolve.

Mini Dissolve

When the next invisible barrier rises, do not fight it. Name it. Soften it. Sashay through it.

That is how you return to yourself, again and again.

Epilogue

Basking in The Afterglow

Every time someone finishes this work, I ask the same question: "What is different now?"

No one ever says, "I'm totally healed," or "I'll never get stuck again." What they say is, "I can come back to myself faster." That is the quiet miracle of The Dissolve.

You do not become superhuman. You simply stop abandoning the human you already are.

Sarah

Sarah still hears Haras whisper sometimes,
but now it makes her smile.

Jonah still feels the tick of the Clock Demon, but
it is background noise, not marching orders.

Maya still feels the Curator tug lightly at her
sleeve, but she brings her into the creative
process instead of locking her out.

Kai still feels The General stiffen his
shoulders on tough days, but now he
recognizes it as loyalty, not threat.

Each of them is still human, still complex,
still alive in motion. But none of them are
ruled by their invisible barriers anymore.
That is the afterglow: not perfection,
but permission and presence.

This Work Is Contagious

The world around you will not change because
you have read this book. Deadlines will still loom.

The inbox will still fill. The world will still spin
too fast. But you will move differently within it.

You will pause when you used to panic.
You will breathe when you used to brace.
You will listen when you used to shout.
You will become the calm in the room that
once fueled your invisible barriers.

And that calm will ripple outward into your team,
your relationships, your art, your leadership.

Because The Dissolve is contagious.

Notice

If something awakened in you as you read,
do not rush to capture it. Just notice it. Let it
hum in the background of your next decision,
your next conversation, your next creation.

Let it remind you that whenever
resistance rises, you have a choice.

You can tighten.

Or you can dissolve.

Your Brilliance

That is all The Dissolve has ever been: A
way home to the version of you that was
never broken. A rhythm you can trust in the
middle of any storm. A conversation between
your brilliance and your tenderness.

You know the language now.

You know the steps.

Go live them.

Mini Dissolve — The Afterglow

Feel your breath. Notice one small area of ease
that was not there before. That is the afterglow.
The proof that you are already moving in rhythm
with yourself.

The Beginning of What Is Next

If something is humming in you as you finish
this book, that is not an accident. That is your
system already recognizing a new way of being.

If you dissolved your way through these pages, you
have already felt the shift. It wasn't inspiration.
It wasn't hype. It was simply recognition.

The Dissolve wakes up something ancient
and practical inside you: your rhythm,
your presence, your capacity to return.
And once you have experienced that even
once, you do not go back. You expand.

But a book can only take you to the threshold.

The next version of you, the one you have been
rehearsing, softening toward, becoming, lives
on the other side of applying this work in real
time. That is where the real beginning is.

So, as you close this chapter, do
not think of it as an ending.

Think of it as the moment you look up from the page and recognize:

I am ready for more.

Now we step into that together.

LET'S CONNECT

If this book resonated... if you saw yourself
in Sarah, Jonah, Maya, Kai, or in any of the
patterns that surfaced... trust that pull.

Your system is telling you something:
You are ready to dissolve differently now.
Not alone. Not theoretically. For real.

Everything I mention here, along
with the free resources from the
appendices, is at **thedissolve.me**.

The Dissolve Year: My Deepest Work

I offer a twelve-month, high-touch
container where you learn to dissolve in
real time, integrate new identity patterns,
and create from your truest self.

We move slow. We move deep. We move with precision. This is where founders, leaders, and world-changing humans come to shift not only their habits, but their entire nervous system relationship to power, presence, and possibility.

If this book opened something in you,
The Dissolve Year is where you live it.
Learn more and apply at thedissolve.me.

The Dissolve Lab: Workshops and Intensives

If you want to experience dissolving in the room, come to a live Dissolve Lab. These are experiential, somatic, high-trust spaces where you:

- Learn the framework
- Practice the steps
- Feel the shift in your body

The first Dissolve Lab will be at SXSW in March 2026.

If you received this book there, you were one of the first fifty people to hold it. Future labs and workshops are announced through my email list and Substack.

The Dissolve Dispatch: My Weekly Notes

If you want to stay connected to the rhythm of this work, join my Substack.

Every week, I send:
- Insights on dissolving in daily life
- Leadership grounded in presence, not pressure
- Stories from the field
- Guided mini dissolves
- Reminders of who you are becoming

It is where the conversation continues between dissolves. Subscribe at thedissolve.me.

The Dissolve Map: Free Download

The Dissolve Map is a visual guide that shows you exactly how to Name, Soften, and Sashay through invisible barriers in real time.

It's simple, elegant, and available to use immediately in your own life. Download it anytime at thedissolve.me.

If This Book Spoke to You, Reach Out

I work with brilliant, driven, world-changing humans who are tired of burning out on their own brilliance. People who want to move from force to flow, from pressure to presence, from survival to creation.

If that is you, let's talk. Call me.
Yes... actually call me.

612-504-2180

You do not need another course. You need a skilled mirror, a clean map, and a companion who knows the terrain of your nervous system and believes deeply in who you are becoming. Let's begin your dissolve.

Acknowledgments

To the clients who trusted me with their inner
worlds, thank you. You know who you are. Your
courage, honesty, humor, and brilliance made this
book possible. The stories of Sarah, Jonah, Maya,
and Kai are composites of you. Your dissolves
shaped these pages as much as my own did.

To the teachers, trainers, leaders, and guides
who expanded my understanding of the human
nervous system and what is possible for it, thank
you. You gave me maps when I was lost, mirrors
when I could not see myself, and moments
that changed my trajectory. Every lesson,
every challenge, every conversation helped me
dissolve patterns that kept me small. I carry
your influence into every room where I teach.

To the teacher whose neuroscience, meditation practices, and mental rehearsal methods transformed my life, thank you. Your work gave me the tools to become a new version of myself and continues to shape everything I create.

To my wife and our littles, you are my greatest reason for dissolving.

You are why I return to myself again and again, why I do my own work with rigor and tenderness, and why I fight for the version of me you deserve, Thank you for loving me through every iteration. Thank you for being the home I come back to.

And to you, the reader, thank you for choosing presence over perfection, curiosity over certainty, and possibility over pressure. Thank you for walking this path with me.

You are the one dissolving now.

I am grateful to witness who you are becoming.

About the Author

Laurie McGinley is a best-selling author, transformation guide, consultant, and keynote speaker who helps ambitious, high-performing people dissolve the invisible barriers that keep them stuck. Known for her clarity, presence, and deep attunement, Laurie works at the intersection of neuroscience, identity, and human potential. She guides founders, leaders, world changers, and creators through transformations that last.

She is a Licensed NeuroChangeSolutions Consultant and has spent years studying, practicing, and embodying the teachings of Dr. Joe Dispenza. Meditation, mental rehearsal, and nervous-system coherence are not abstract concepts to her. They are lived disciplines woven into the fabric of her life and teaching.

Before becoming a coach, Laurie was a Division I distance runner, a designer, a strategist, and a lifelong student of what it means to lead without armor. She is a Licensed Architect who no longer practices. Her own dissolves, personal and hard-earned, formed the foundation of the method you now hold in your hands.

Laurie is the creator of The Dissolve, a framework used by leaders and teams across industries to break old patterns, soften inner resistance, and move through challenges with clarity and ease. She teaches this work in one-on-one coaching, in organizations, and inside The Dissolve Year, her signature yearlong program for those ready to create without limits.

When she is not working with clients or teaching this material, Laurie can be found innovating The Dissolve in her own life, woodturning as meditation, and genuinely enjoying the feeling of running super fast.

To learn more or begin your own dissolve, visit **thedissolve.me**.

Exercise 1

How To Dissolve In 90 Seconds

If you want to keep this close, you can download a printable version and a phone lock screen of the 90 Second Dissolve at thedissolve.me.

This is the condensed practice. The entire framework in one minute and a half. Use it anywhere. In traffic. Before a meeting. Mid meltdown. Mid breakthrough.

STEP 1: Name It (30 seconds)

Notice what is happening. Do not overthink. Just ask, "Who is here right now?"

Invisible barriers always have a tone.
Harsh. Panicked. Moral. Urgent.
Intellectual. Charming. Quiet.

Say its name gently.

"Hey, Clock Demon."

"Hi, Haras."

"I see you, General."

No judgment. Just recognition.

STEP 2: Soften It (30 seconds)

Drop your shoulders.

Unclench your jaw.

Let your tongue fall from the roof of your mouth.

Breathe out longer than you breathe in.

Let your body register safety even
if your mind still doubts it.

This is where the grip loosens.

STEP 3: Sashay Through It (30 seconds)

Get curious about how Future You
would respond in this situation.

Feel Future You in your body.

Sit with them.

Trust that you can feel that way too.

No forcing. Just rehearsing ease.

That is it. Ninety seconds. Your nervous
system will remember this practice
faster than your mind does.

Exercise 2

Questions for Team Leaders

Using The Dissolve to Build Regulated, Creative, High-Trust Teams

Cultures change when leaders change the rhythm. And The Dissolve gives you the map.

If you would like a printable version of these questions to use in your next team meeting or offsite, you can download the Dissolve for Teams worksheet at thedissolve.me.

The Dissolve is not only a personal practice. It is a leadership strategy. When leaders dissolve in real time, teams feel it.

Meetings shorten. Decisions get cleaner. People stop bracing. Creativity comes back online.

These questions are designed for founders, managers, and executives who want to build cultures rooted in presence instead of pressure, and rhythm instead of reactivity.

Use them in one-on-ones, team reflections, off-sites, Level 10s, or executive coaching conversations.

1. AWARENESS

See the invisible currents shaping your culture.

- Where does pressure hide in our team culture such as deadlines, silence, speed, tone, or hierarchy?
- What invisible rules govern how we "should" behave here, even if no one says them out loud?
- What emotions or reactions do people feel they must hide at work?
- What happens in the moment before we rush to a solution? Do we notice it, or do we override it?

- Are we rewarding output or presence? Activity or awareness? Motion or momentum?
- Awareness tells the truth about what is actually running the team, not what leadership hopes is running it.

2. SOFTENING

Model calm so others can access their best thinking.

- How do I personally show my team what regulated leadership looks like in chaos? How do I model The Dissolve?
- Where am I bracing, tightening, controlling, or over-functioning? What would softening look like instead?
- What would happen if I paused for one breath before responding, deciding, or redirecting?
- How could we normalize rest, space, and stillness as part of high performance instead of the opposite of it?
- When tension rises in a room, how do I embody The Dissolve and signal safety?

Softening is contagious. When the leader
stays open, the team stays intelligent.

3. MOVEMENT

Shift from urgency to rhythm, from force to flow.

- What does flow look like for our team, not
  theoretically but in real daily work?
- Where are we moving too fast to think clearly
  or too slow to stay alive?
- How can we make decisions with rhythm
  instead of urgency?
- What meetings or processes could move with
  less friction and more clarity?
- How can we celebrate progress that feels alive
  such as creative, integrated, and embodied,
  rather than simply productive?

Teams that move with rhythm move with trust.
And trust accelerates everything that matters.

For Teams Who Want to Go Further

When a team learns to dissolve
together, they unlock:

- Clearer communication
- More honest conversations
- Fewer emergency meetings
- Decisions that stick
- Reduced emotional reactivity
- Higher creativity and capacity
- Leadership that feels grounded instead
  of grinding

Exercise 3

The Invisible Barriers Bank

Common governors by Enneagram type. These are not diagnoses. They are mirrors. Use them to recognize your own patterns and language.

One: The Perfectionist (Sarah)

- The Auditor: "Do better."
- The Judge: "You should know this already."
- The Martyr: "If it is not hard, it is not holy."
- The Shadow Saint: "You can rest after it is perfect."

Three: The Hero (Jonah)

- The Clock Demon: "You are already behind."
- The Performer: "If you stop, they will forget you."
- The Strategist: "You can rest after the win."
- The Mirror Maker: "You are only as good as their reaction."

Five: The Researcher (Maya)

- The Curator: "Do not share until it is flawless."
- The Archivist: "Gather more data first."
- The Gatekeeper: "You will be misunderstood."
- The Hermit: "It is safer alone."

Eight: The Motivator (Kai)

- The General: "If you do not command, you will lose control."
- The Sentinel: "Vulnerability is weakness."
- The Enforcer: "If I relax, others will fail."
- The Fortress: "Power means protection, not connection."

Each barrier protects something sacred: your original gift. Every governor guards a genius.

If you would like support working with your specific invisible barrier, you will find ways to work with me at thedissolve.me.

Exercise 4

Book Club Guide

If you are hosting a book club or reading group, you can download a printable Book Club Kit (including this guide, a host outline, and an invite template) at thedissolve.me.

This guide is designed for groups who want to experience The Dissolve together, not analyze it.

The goal is not to interpret the book. The goal is to apply it gently, honestly, and in real time.

Each session includes:
- Opening grounding
- Core reflections
- Embodied questions

- Optional practices
- A closing prompt for integration

Use one session per week or spread them out. Keep in mind, what matters is the rhythm, not the speed.

SESSION 1: The Anatomy of Stuck

Seeing the invisible is the first dissolve.

Opening Grounding

One breath together. Inhale awareness. Exhale pressure.

Core Reflections
- Where do you feel stuckness show up most often: at work, in relationships, in creativity, or in leadership?
- What invisible barrier resonated most with you: The Clock Demon, The Curator, The General, The Gilded Dustpan, The Veil, The Escape Artist, The Over Crusher, etc.?
- Which character (Sarah, Jonah, Maya, Kai) felt most familiar to you and why?

Embodied Questions

- When you get stuck, what happens in your body first?
- What do you habitually do next: rush, withdraw, analyze, control, or try to prove something?

Optional Practice

Notice one stuck pattern in the next 48 hours. Do not change it. Simply witness it.

Closing Prompt

What does "stuck" actually feel like in your body, not as a concept but as a sensation?

SESSION 2: Name It

Language reveals the pattern.

Opening Grounding

Place a hand on your chest and come into your body. Where does your pattern speak?

Core Reflections
- What is the name of your invisible barrier?
- How did you know the name was right?
- What does naming it change for you?

Embodied Questions
- What happens in your body when you say the name out loud?
- Does the pattern feel louder, smaller, clearer, or more distant?

Optional Practice

Write one sentence your invisible barrier often whispers to you. Then write one sentence you want to whisper back.

Closing Prompt

What truth did naming your invisible barrier reveal about who you are becoming?

SESSION 3: Soften It

Softening is intelligence, not surrender.

Opening Grounding

One slow breath into the rib cage.
One slow breath out.

Core Reflections
- What does softening look like in your daily life: physically, emotionally, and mentally?
- What did Sarah, Jonah, Maya, and Kai teach you about softening through their stories?
- Where in your life does your body still believe tension equals control?

Embodied Questions
- When you soften, which old habits protest?
- What sensations show up when your nervous system begins to downshift?

Optional Practice

Choose one place to practice softening before reacting. This could be a meeting, an email, a conversation, or a decision.

Closing Prompt

What surprised you when you softened something you normally force?

SESSION 4: Sashay Through It

Rehearsal creates identity. Rhythm creates change.

Opening Grounding

Imagine yourself two steps ahead of where
you are now. Who are you becoming?

Core Reflections
- What future version of yourself are you
  rehearsing?
- What would moving with rhythm look like
  inside your current challenge?
- What part of Sashay resonates most with you:
  intention, mental rehearsal, or embodiment?

Embodied Questions
- What emotion does your future self feel easily
  that you struggle to feel now?
- What is one place in your week where you
  could rehearse being that version of you?

Optional Practice

Go to thedissolve.me and use the short meditation
I share with my clients to mentally rehearse
for a situation where you normally brace.

Closing Prompt

How did imagining your future self shift
how you feel in your current life?

SESSION 5: Dissolving in Real Time

Where the work becomes instinct.

Opening Grounding

Notice your inhale. Notice your exhale. Return.

Core Reflections
- Share one real-time dissolve moment from
  your week.
- What did you notice in your body the
  moment the old loop tried to take over?
- How did awareness shift the outcome, even
  slightly?

Embodied Questions
- Which step of The Dissolve felt hardest for
  you: naming, softening, or sashaying?
- What does returning to yourself mean in your
  lived experience?

Optional Practice

Choose a recurring moment such as a meeting, a morning routine, a commute, or a conflict point.

Intentionally dissolve one small
pattern there this week.

Closing Prompt

Now that you have walked The Dissolve, what does creation without limits mean to you?

Exercise 5

Dissolve Journal Prompts

If you would like these prompts in a printable journal format, you can download the Dissolve Journal PDF at thedissolve.me.

These prompts help you move from understanding The Dissolve to living it.

Use them slowly, honestly, and gently. Your nervous system will guide you if you let it.

I. STUCKNESS + INVISIBLE BARRIERS

Before dissolving anything, learn to see what is running the show.

- When do you notice yourself tightening, bracing, rushing, or withdrawing?
- What situation or relationship reliably activates your oldest pattern?
- What does "stuck" actually feel like in your body: throat, chest, stomach, or jaw?
- What do you believe about yourself in those moments?
- Who taught you that this behavior kept you safe?

II. NAME IT

Language reveals what your body already knows.
- What name feels true for your invisible barrier (The Clock Demon, The Curator, The General, The Gilded Dustpan, The Over Crusher, The Caffeinated Manager, etc.)?
- What is the sentence your governor whispers most often?
- How does your body react the moment you say the barrier's name out loud?
- What is your barrier trying to protect you from?
- What version of you does it not trust yet?

III. SOFTEN IT

Softening is not surrender. It
is regulated attention.
- Where in your body do you brace most often,
  and when did that become your default?
- What do you fear would happen if you relaxed
  your grip even slightly?
- What is one place in your day where tension
  feels automatic but unnecessary?
- When have you softened recently, even
  without meaning to?
- What evidence do you have that softness
  brings better results than force?

IV. SASHAY THROUGH IT

Rehearsal creates identity. Rhythm creates
change. You can find the meditation I use
with my clients at thedissolve.me. This is
very effective when paired with writing.
- Who is the future version of yourself you are
  rehearsing?
- What thoughts, emotions, and sensations
  belong to that version of you?
- What would moving with rhythm look like
  inside your current challenge?

- Where could you allow flow today instead of force?
- What is one small and elegant step your future self would take right now?

V. DISSOLVING IN REAL TIME
- This is where The Dissolve becomes instinct.
- Where did you catch yourself dissolving this week, even briefly?
- What moment brought up an old reaction, and how did you move through it differently?
- What situation surprised you because you stayed present instead of spiraling?
- What did awareness give you access to: clarity, compassion, creativity, or choice?
- What rhythm is emerging in your life now that presence is possible?

VI. RETURNING TO YOURSELF

Freedom is not perfection. It
is the ability to return.
- When you forget the steps, how do you find your way back?
- What part of you feels safest when you are present?
- What part of you still resists softening, and why?

- What is becoming easier that once felt impossible?
- What does creation without limits mean to you right now?

VII. THE NEXT BECOMING

Identity expands in the direction of your attention.
- Who are you becoming as you dissolve these patterns?
- What qualities are you noticing more often in yourself: steadiness, openness, courage, or ease?
- How is your relationship to power changing?
- What do you want your life to feel like one year from now?
- What is your next invisible barrier inviting you to learn?

CONTACT

If this book resonates with you and you're ready to get started you can find me at **thedissolve.me** or by calling me at 612-504-2180.